Praise for
GRAY DAY

"If Robert Ludlum spitballed an espionage story with a Russian hacker, they might have conjured up something as wild and riveting as *Gray Day*. Except that this yarn, incredibly, is true. An enthralling spy tale that feels ever more relevant with each passing day."

—DAVE HOWARD, author of *Chasing Phil:*
The Adventures of Two Undercover Agents
with the World's Most Charming Con Man

"What job could possibly be more twisty, mind-bending, and demanding than being an undercover spy in one of the FBI's own cybersecurity units? With resolute doggedness, shrewd psychological instincts, and the sheer guts to make critical split-second decisions, rookie agent Eric O'Neill helped to turn the tables on his own boss—one of the most dangerous traitors of our time. In *Gray Day* he weaves together his personal and professional stories with all the skills of a seasoned novelist. The result is a thrilling, page-turning brew worthy of Hollywood—only better because it's real."

—ELISABETH ELO, author of
Finding Katarina M.

"*Gray Day* is a fascinating read about catching infamous spymaster Robert Hanssen, who turned over classified materials to the Russians. You can't help but root for O'Neill as he tells his story of spying on the spymaster. I recommend this gripping book to all audiences, especially computer geeks and those interested in cybersecurity."

—KEVIN MITNICK, *New York Times*
bestselling author of *Ghost in the Wires*
and *The Art of Invisibility*

"An adrenaline-laced memoir . . . as compulsively readable as any thriller. O'Neill has a knack for ratcheting up tension so that foregone historical conclusions, such as Hanssen's capture, feel like white-knuckle cliffhangers. . . . O'Neill's page-turner deglamorizes undercover work while conveying the uncertainty, stress, and excitement that accompany a successful investigation."

—*Publishers Weekly*

"A taut and compelling real-life thriller . . . Part memoir, part true crime, this fast-paced work is recommended for anyone interested in cybersecurity, Cold War history, and espionage tales."

—*Library Journal*

"O'Neill's narrative . . . is valuable in its exploration of the psychology of the traitor and his motivations as well as how spies like Hanssen so often enjoy success for as long as they do until finally caught: 'Amateurs may hack machines, but professionals hack people.' Fans of spy fiction and true crime will find plenty to enjoy in O'Neill's account."

—*Kirkus Reviews*

GRAY DAY

My Undercover Mission to

Expose America's

First Cyber Spy

ERIC O'NEILL

B\D\W\Y
Broadway Books
New York

Copyright © 2019 by Eric M. O'Neill

Published in the United States by Broadway Books, an imprint of Random House, a division of Penguin Random House LLC, New York.

crownpublishing.com

BROADWAY BOOKS and its logo, B \ D \ W \ Y, are trademarks of Penguin Random House LLC.

Originally published in hardcover in the United States by Crown, an imprint of Random House, a division of Penguin Random House LLC, New York, in 2019.

LIBRARY OF CONGRESS CATALOGING-IN-PUBLICATION DATA
Names: O'Neill, Eric, author.
Title: Gray day: my undercover mission to expose America's first cyber spy / Eric O'Neill.
Description: First edition. | New York: Crown Publishers, 2019.
Identifiers: LCCN 2018038605 (print) | LCCN 2018048826 (ebook) | ISBN 9780525573548 (ebook) | ISBN 9780525573524 (hardback) | ISBN 9780525573531 (paperback)
Subjects: LCSH: Hanssen, Robert. | O'Neill, Eric. | United States. Federal Bureau of Investigation. | Cyber intelligence (Computer security) | Spies—Russia (Federation)—Biography. | Spies—United States—Biography. | Intelligence service—United States. | BISAC: POLITICAL SCIENCE / Political Freedom & Security / Intelligence. | BIOGRAPHY & AUTOBIOGRAPHY / Personal Memoirs. | COMPUTERS / Security / Viruses.
Classification: LCC UB271.R92 (ebook) | LCC UB271.R92 H37153 2019 (print) | DDC 327.1247073092 [B]—dc23
LC record available at https://lccn.loc.gov/2018038605

ISBN 978-0-525-57353-1
Ebook ISBN 978-0-525-57354-8

Printed in the United States of America

Book design by Lauren Dong

First Paperback Edition

To my mother, Vivian
The bravest person I've ever known

Contents

GRAY
DAY

CHAPTER 1

TIPPING POINTS

December 10, 2000—Sunday

Phones should not ring on Sunday mornings. I rolled across the bed, scooped my battered Nokia from the nightstand, and burrowed back under the covers. Our English basement apartment reminded me of winter camping trips I'd gone on as a Boy Scout. The single-pane windows trapped about as much heat as a canvas tent.

Juliana peered at me over the thick comforter. Her eyes were glazed with sleep, and her blond hair was piled around her head like windblown thistle. We'd been married four months, and each morning I woke beside her was a revelation. I checked the time—8:00 a.m. I was about to slap the phone down on the receiver when the voice on the other end made me freeze. All thoughts of a lazy morning flushed out of my mind. It was Supervisory Special Agent Gene McClelland.

"Don't bother getting dressed up," he said. "Just lace up your shoes. I'm parked out front."

As I fumbled for my pants, my mind raced through possible scenarios, all of them grim. It was unheard-of for an FBI supervisor, the man in charge of my entire squad, to show up at a private residence on a Sunday morning. To put this into perspective, imagine your boss—the president or manager of your company—arriving at your house early one weekend morning. If you are the boss, imagine the chairman of your board parked in your driveway. If you are the chairman, imagine POTUS himself dropping by, waiting for you to appear. This was worse than any of that.

FBI supervisors never come to you. They summon. Gene showing up at my apartment could only mean something was wrong. I pulled a George Washington University Law sweatshirt over my head and took a deep breath. "No idea what's going on, but Gene is parked outside." The concern on Juliana's face made me pause. "I'll be right back." Then I swallowed my hollow words and turned to leave.

I eased through the front door out onto the sparse lawn. Number 626 was only a few steps away from E Street, and a quick jog away from the US Capitol Building. Our building squatted between expensive town houses like an ugly sibling in a family portrait. The crammed one-bedroom sometimes felt like a closet, and we'd found mold behind the walls and in the lone heater, but it was all we could afford.

As the wind hit my face, I looked up. No one on the surrounding rooftops or balconies. I did a quick lateral scan and saw the red splash of a cardinal light upon a telephone wire. A runner huffed his Spandexed way down E Street, and the distant noise of traffic droned from nearby Pennsylvania Avenue like waves on a beach. Only one car I didn't recognize was parked on the street. Gene.

Each step away from the building made me wince, but no SWAT vans came crashing around the corner, sirens blazing. Instead, the window of the idling sedan rolled down. "Get in," Gene said.

I slid into the passenger seat and closed the door against the December chill.

Gene didn't bother with niceties. "Have you ever heard of Robert Hanssen?"

I hadn't. "Should I have?" I asked.

"No," Gene smiled. "That's good."

I nodded.

"That's why we chose you."

I stayed silent, trying to parse the insult from the compliment. The only certainty was that I'd been left in the dark—again. For months now, I hadn't been able to pursue any of my normal, high-priority targets for the FBI. I'd been slapped on the wrist, shuffled into the minor league. Not because I'd messed up a lead or bungled a case, but because I'd married Juliana—a German national.

No one had told me that FBI operatives with high security clearance are required to fill out a permission form *before* proposing to the love of their life. The FBI had instituted the policy after a few agents married into the mob. Meet the perfect girl, marry her, and then learn that her father is an FBI organized-crime target. Not the brightest moments for the universe's premier investigative agency.

Still, imagine my shock when I bounced into the office to let my team know that I'd proposed marriage to the most wonderful girl, and my supervisor asked after my engagement form.

Then imagine me telling the FBI brass that my new bride hailed from Brandenburg, Germany. Faces that were rarely cheerful turned to stone. "You should have reported contact with an East German national," they said.

"Don't you mean German national?" I asked. "Haven't you heard of reunification? There is no more East Germany."

"Not to us."

The FBI benched me while the FBI legat, or legal attaché office, in Germany investigated my in-laws. Think of a whale trapped on a sandy beach desperate to get back into the water. That was me. I sat in the office day after day with a suspended security clearance, working on a target-acquisition database I'd developed, until the FBI convinced itself that Juliana was not a spy. The investigation into Juliana's family occurred before I had a chance to meet them, and I'm still pretty convinced my in-laws think I'm Stasi. They aren't far off.

By this point I'd been in the FBI nearly five years working as an investigative specialist, otherwise known as an "investigator," but better known as a ghost. Not too many years before I typed up my FBI application, the agency realized that Russian targets could run circles around special agents, who focused on criminal investigations and technological and research-based counterintelligence. This was especially the case just after World War II, when a target could look over his shoulder and see a legion of buzz-cut, well-suited white males swarming him. Not exactly subtle. Without specialized surveillance and undercover investigative training, the agents were at a constant disadvantage: the Russians had more operatives and better tradecraft. The FBI was stuck solving crimes after the fact, when what it needed to do was stop the spies before they committed those crimes.

The special agents were already overburdened. So the agency decided to try something new. In the age-old tradition of American innovation, we traveled back across the pond to learn how MI5 handles surveillance in the United Kingdom through a specialized group called the Watchers. MI5's secretive group had elevated surveillance to an art form. Nothing would stand between a Watcher and his target. A story I once heard placed two Watchers in a canoe floating within a murky water tower, watching their target through a hole drilled in the tower's metal shell. There were a lot of stories like that. The FBI took everything the Watchers could do and made it better. The ghosts were born.

My training allowed me to follow a person from sunup to sundown, know what he ate for breakfast, and count how many times he tied his shoes or checked his watch. I could track each smile, know whom he met or whom he tried to avoid, log where he went and how he got there and everything in between. I'd learn his tradecraft and look like I'd practiced it longer than he had. I was a professional driver and photographer, didn't need to sleep, and could stare at a single door for hours, just waiting for him to walk through.

My dark brown hair, hazel eyes, and slightly olive complexion—a gift from my Italian mother—meant that I could easily pass for a number of ethnicities, and thanks to my father's burly genes, I could grow a beard in a matter of days. I was a master of disguise, of social engineering, of sweet-talking my way past situations. I had a badge but never used it. A target might see me a dozen times across a day's work, but he wouldn't notice me. I was trained to blend into situations, to find cover in plain sight, to look unobtrusive, uninteresting, and unremarkable. I'd call in a spy before he spied or committed an act of terrorism, then melt into the shadows while he was still wondering where all the FBI agents had suddenly come from. I knew how to be gray.

"Who's Hanssen?" I asked.

Gene shrugged. "We think he's a spy. We want you to investigate him."

It took me a moment to get the words past my teeth. "Gene. You woke me up on a Sunday morning, dragged me out of bed, scared the hell out of me by coming here, all to ask me to do my job? Couldn't this have waited until Monday?"

Gene shook his head. "We don't want you to ghost him, Eric. We want you to investigate him. Face-to-face."

I sat there, frozen.

"We need someone on the ground with him," Gene explained. "To develop a relationship, try to get some dirt. I've recommended you."

I opened and closed my mouth like a guppy gasping for oxygen. Gene had asked me to participate in what amounted to an elicitation operation—one where the undercover asset engages in conversation, memorizes details, learns facts, and draws out information. I'd been involved in high-risk cases, but I'd never been instructed to interact with a target face-to-face; my job was to play a backstage part out of sightlines. For the first time, Gene was asking me to play myself. I probably did look like a fish—one miles away from water.

"I need your answer. In or out."

There are tipping points in every life. Tiny moments in time when we're forced to make a choice: take the leap or stand by and let the opportunity pass. These are the moments that shape a future.

This was one of mine.

"What do I tell Juliana?"

Gene scratched his head. "I dunno. Tell her you got promoted. You'll be assigned to a computer job at headquarters." His eyes hardened. "I don't have to tell you to keep the rest quiet. As far as you are concerned, the only people that know about this are you and me. Juliana can't know anything."

I got it. Although Juliana knew I worked for the FBI, we had a deal never to discuss it. She once told me that she enjoyed having a husband who never spoke about work. We'd talk about other things—hopes and dreams, the drama her fellow business students got up to, our long-running debate about whether American football was better than European soccer—but never about what I did all day.

"Gene," I said. "I'm keying in on the word 'promotion.' If I really need to sell this . . ." Now I was the one smiling.

"Okay, okay, Eric." Gene's short chuckle faded into a cough. "I'll get you some extra overtime. You'll more than earn it." He put the car into drive. "In or out."

I leapt.

Target: Robert Hanssen

Suspected spy

CHAPTER 2

THE TYRANNY OF SECRETS

There is no such thing as a lie detector. Despite numerous advances in behavioral science and technology, a person cannot use facial expressions or verbal "tells" to sniff out a lie with a great deal of certainty. Nor can a machine measure the thoughts that speed through a person's mind.

How do crack investigators sort lies from truth when they have a suspect in the interview chair? They combine a little psychology, a little technology, and a dash of Hollywood stagecraft. The standard polygraph machine measures pulse, blood pressure, respiration, and skin conductivity while a person is asked specific questions. Today these metrics are graphed on a computer screen, but in the past the machine scratched ink across an ever-expanding roll of graph paper. In theory, a deceptive response to a particular question will spike some or all of the physiological indicators—a quickened pulse, a sweaty palm.

But the machine is not infallible, and accurate results require an expert examiner. Spies have developed many ploys and countermeasures to defeat the machine. An old story about Russian spymasters stands out: When American moles were being trained by their Russian handlers to make dead drops and other clandestine exchanges, the Russian intelligence officer in charge provided advice on how to defeat a US intelligence agency's standard polygraph. One such countermeasure, typical of Russia's often brutal espionage tactics, was to step on a tack that the spy had hidden in the toe of his shoe during the examination. The severe pain would provide a necessary physiological spike at tactical moments in order to fool the examiner.

To join the FBI as a counterintelligence investigator, I needed to receive a top-secret security clearance. And to do that, I needed to pass a polygraph.

Of course, I didn't have a tack in my shoe during my first examination. The FBI called me into a gloomy room in a nondescript office building sandwiched between a coffee shop and a shoe store. A man in shirtsleeves and a tie—security badge on a lanyard around his neck and a pile of paperwork on his lap—sat me in a chair facing the door. With practiced motions, he fit a thick band across the midpoint of my chest, right at my diaphragm, and clipped sensors onto the fingers of my right hand. A blood-pressure cuff squeezed my upper arm. Numerous wires and cables trailed from the various attachments on my body to a metal box on a side table. Nothing about the situation made me comfortable.

The questions he asked made me recall an initial step in my background investigation—half a year before I ended up strapped in the polygraph chair. One Sunday morning after I first applied to the FBI, a retired agent had shown up unannounced at the town house I shared with three roommates. I was in my early twenties, and when the doorbell rang, I was sitting on the couch with an old friend, recovering after a wild Saturday night. Christian and I had known each other since we were ten. After over a decade of friendship, he knew where I hid my skeletons.

The agent who appeared on that Sunday morning hoped to interview my roommates—a standard part of the background-check process. When he learned that my housemates were out, he pointed toward Christian and said, "Who's that?"

"My best friend of ten years," I said.

The agent smiled. "He'll do." He looked at me. "Why don't you go upstairs for a while?"

An hour later, I rejoined Christian on the couch. My old friend answered my impatience with a perplexed face.

"Strange questions," he said.

"Like what?"

" 'Have you ever known Eric to injure or torture small animals or seek their death?' "

We both had a chuckle at that one. The next question was about my relationship with money. Was I frugal or a spendthrift? Did I have a gambling problem, or take risks with money, or seem to go through large amounts of it?

No worries there either.

"The third question though . . ." He paused. " 'Has he ever been known to drink excessively, or have a problem with alcohol, or drink more than a few alcoholic drinks in any one day?' "

I pressed my palms into my eyes and pushed away the lingering headache from the party the night before.

"What did you say?"

He grinned and shrugged. Probably the same expressions he'd used with the agent. "No more than anyone else I know."

In that moment, I thought my best friend had doomed me to never make it into the FBI. I'd flunk my security clearance, get a form letter thanking me for my interest, and have to go find a desk job at some consulting firm that would suck away at my soul, hour by hour.

Instead, I passed. It probably helped that I'm an Eagle Scout, have never touched an illegal drug in my life, and come from a line of upstanding attorneys and military officers. Whatever the case, I finally found myself in a polygraph examination, the last step before securing the clearance that would start my new career, again doubting I'd pass.

"Stop whatever it is you're doing," the examiner said. "You're doing something with your breathing that will get you an inconclusive. I can't pass you with an inconclusive. I don't pass you, you don't get into the FBI."

I focused on my breath. I'd studied martial arts for the majority of my life, which meant I'd learned to control my breathing to reduce stress and promote calmness. But for the polygraph to work, the examiner needed to create stress to establish my normal patterns. I had to unlearn years of study, stat.

I also had to lie. The tester needed to catch me in an easy falsehood so that he could establish a baseline when he got to the questions that actually mattered to him. The problem for both of us was that I didn't have much to lie about. When it came to the kinds of youthful indiscretions polygraph examiners tend to ask about—stealing candy bars, smoking pot, cheating on tests—I was clean as a whistle.

Then he asked me if I'd ever lied to someone who loves me. He prefaced the question by making it clear, in no uncertain terms, that if I had, he would fail me. I pictured my mother. Over the past five years, Parkinson's disease had drawn her ready smile into a perpetual frown. A few days earlier, she'd asked me how she looked, and I'd said, "Perfect." It was the first lie I'd ever told her.

The polygraph examiner scrutinized me. "No," I answered. The needle raced across the page, the first rapid movement since the examination began. The examiner had his baseline. His next question was whether a foreign national had ever approached me to request anything, or to ask about my application to the FBI. I relaxed and answered "no." The needle ceased its furious scribbling and found the center of the page. I passed.

The intelligence community initiates new members into a tyranny of secrets. It is within this mind-set that spies and counterintelligence operatives—those who hunt the spies before they can steal, disrupt, or spread disinformation—operate. The two most important rules for a spy: don't get caught; and if compromised, lie. A counterintelligence operative follows a similar but far more difficult mandate: say nothing about your secrets. But just as in the biblical story of Adam and Eve, eating from the tree of knowledge can have unintended consequences, and a secret can corrode from within.

Some scholars claim that Tsar Ivan IV Vasilyevich, also known as Ivan the Terrible, established Russia's first spy services in the sixteenth century. But it was during the Cold War that the Soviet Union turned espionage into an art form. Russian spymasters launched massive collection campaigns to recruit American moles from within the FBI, CIA, and NSA. At the same time, they were pioneering *desinformatsiya* practices that spread disinformation and disruption in order to shape American political decisions. These active-measure (*aktivinyye meropriatia*) disinformation campaigns included media manipulation; use of front organizations (like the US affiliate of the World Peace Council, a secret Soviet affiliate) to sway public opinion; kidnappings; and provision of funds, training, and support to terrorist organizations, to name a few. In 1980, the CIA estimated that the Soviets spent a conservative $3 billion per year pursuing active measures. In his February 6, 1980, congressional testimony, John McMahon, the CIA deputy director for operations, stated that the Soviets' active-measures network was "second to none in comparison to the major world powers in its size and effectiveness."

The 1980s saw a number of audacious—and highly successful—disinformation campaigns. One involved spreading rumors of CIA and FBI involvement in President John F. Kennedy's assassination. Another seeded foreign newspapers with articles—purportedly written by American scientists—claiming that AIDS was the result of the Pentagon's experiments to develop biological weapons. During the 1984 Summer Olympics in Los Angeles, KGB spies in Washington, DC, sent fake letters from the KKK threatening athletes from African countries, an active measure many believe was a response to President Jimmy Carter's boycott of the 1980 Moscow Games.

Yet for all its successes abroad, the Soviet Union was suffering from serious internal tensions. In the late 1980s, massive independence protests swept across the Caucasus and the Baltic states, and soon the USSR's constituent republics began to secede. On August 18, 1991, military and government hardliners staged a coup against Mikhail Gorbachev. The coup collapsed within days, but the match continued to burn. In December 1991, Gorbachev announced the dissolution of the Soviet Union and his resignation as president. Television audiences across the former USSR watched as Boris Yeltsin lowered the hammer-and-sickle flag from atop the Kremlin for the last time and raised the tricolor flag as president of a newly independent Russian state.

During all this upheaval, former KGB spymasters—now out of a job—were raiding the agency's file cabinets. The documents they stole would serve as insurance policies for better lives elsewhere. For many, that meant the United States, which offered Levi's jeans, Diet Cokes—and what often amounted to millions of dollars in exchange for the slim files they gave to the FBI. The United States gobbled up their secrets, and the United Kingdom and other friendly intelligence services caught what we missed. The FBI and MI6 pooled the information they'd obtained, which led to a series of arrests of Russian assets within the United States. The biggest catch was Aldrich Ames, a CIA analyst turned KGB mole, whose disclosures had led to the death of many CIA and FBI assets overseas. When asked how he'd passed CIA polygraph tests during his spy career, Ames had laughed: "Confidence and a friendly rapport with the examiner." But as damaging as Ames was, his espionage couldn't account for all of the US intelligence operations that had failed without warning. Someone was continuing to corrupt the intelligence community. Someone even worse than Ames.

The intelligence community had long sought a Russian mole code-named "Gray Suit." Every ghost on the street hoped that the spy they were following might turn out to be him. He was our Billy the Kid, our Blackbeard. And so far, he'd eluded the FBI's best spy catchers. That didn't stop us from hunting.

In the meantime, FBI counterintelligence units had mountains of leads to follow thanks to the former KGB defectors. My commission as an FBI investigative specialist had come just as the agency was sorting through those leads, and months before the FBI Academy in Quantico, Virginia, had an open bunk in its National Security School. Without proper training, I couldn't be set loose in the field to hunt spies and terrorists. But the FBI could assign me to a squad of agents as part of an active espionage investigation—which is how, a little over a year after graduating from college, I ended up part of the mission to capture Earl Edwin Pitts, Russian spy and former FBI agent.

In 1995, the FBI's Washington Field Office commanded the top floors of a federal office building on the banks of the Anacostia River. The spectacularly ugly building, aptly located at Buzzard Point in Southwest Washington, DC, almost made me regret joining the FBI. But the team of agents, led by legendary spy hunter Mike Donner, quickly won me over.

A thirteen-year FBI veteran, Pitts had spied for the Soviet Union from 1987 until 1992. He first volunteered his services to the Soviet Union in July 1987 by sending a letter to a member of the Soviet Mission assigned to the United Nations in New York City. Pitts's new contact soon introduced him to Alexsandr Vasilyevich Karpov, the Soviet Line KR chief for New York, at a clandestine meet at the New York Public Library. Line KR, the counterintelligence unit of the KGB, was responsible for recruiting spies from foreign nations. The FBI learned of Pitts's treachery in 1995, when his original Soviet contact defected to the United States and became a confidential witness against him.

The accusations against Pitts created a problem for the Justice Department, which was tasked with prosecuting the case. In general, securing an espionage conviction requires the government to prove that the spy willfully handed information that was classified or related to national defense over to a foreign nation or other party seeking to harm the United States, and that he or she did so with reason to believe the information would harm the United States or help a foreign nation. It's easier to prove conspiracy to commit espionage, which requires only that the spy *intended* to provide classified information to a foreign power, and that he or she committed some act to further the espionage.

But when it came to the Pitts case, even making out the conspiracy charge was going to be a challenge. While the confidential witness had pointed an unshaking finger at Pitts, a first-year law student could see that the government's case against him was flimsy: it relied entirely on circumstantial information handed over by a defector in return for money and a new life in America. The confidential witness would disappear into Witness Protection and never testify to the evidence on the stand. A good defense attorney could easily raise enough questions about the witness's motives to secure a "not guilty" verdict. The FBI needed Pitts to confess.

In order to make that happen, the bureau created a compartmentalized squad of agents to run what's known as a "false flag" operation. In August 1995, the FBI used the confidential witness, alongside a team of FBI agents led by Donner and posing as Russian intelligence officers, to fool Pitts into believing that Russia wanted to reactivate him as a spy. The false flag operation lasted sixteen months. During that time, Pitts made twenty-two drops of classified and unclassified FBI information and documents, held two face-to-face meetings and nine phone conversations with his pretend Russian handlers, and accepted payment of $65,000 for his attempted espionage. Donner's squad had measured out plenty of rope for Pitts to hang himself.

I joined Donner's squad in the final few months of that investigation, probably because Donner heard I knew how to turn on a computer. Whatever the reason, I couldn't believe my luck. I'd joined the FBI to hunt spies and make a difference. Now, here I was, assigned to the FBI's biggest and most secretive case. I felt like a high school baseball player asked to warm up in the Oriole bullpen with a promise that the team might give me a shot at the big show. The first time I walked into the squad room, I could barely croak out a hello.

Of course, the FBI doesn't throw a twenty-two-year-old future investigator into the path of a spy. My role was to shadow the agents, learn counterintelligence from them, and organize the evidence they collected against Pitts into a computer database. But before I could even consider pressing my thumb against the biometric scanner that sheltered the Pitts squad from the rest of the FBI, I required further initiation into the tyranny of secrets.

A common misconception, even within the intelligence community, is that there are multiple levels of clearance above top secret. In reality, the top clearance is top secret/special compartmentalized intelligence, or TS/SCI. This phrase may seem cryptic, but those familiar with best practices for securing information will recognize its meaning. The idea is to section off critical information—the kind of information that could jeopardize an investigation or harm national security if it fell into the wrong hands—into "compartments," each accessible only to those who need to know that specific information in order to do their jobs. To join the squad investigating Earl Pitts, I needed to attend additional security briefings so that the FBI could grant me access to two additional compartments: Special Intelligence (SI) and Talent Keyhole (TK) intelligence. SI covers communication intercepts, such as listening in to and analyzing and decoding foreign military radio-traffic, and TK protects signals intelligence (or SIGINT), which might include target data spotted by a reconnaissance satellite. Because I would potentially have access to information derived from these compartments during the Earl Pitts investigation, the FBI had to initiate me into the relevant circles of trust.

If this sounds like a lot to handle, it is. Every investigation involves different intelligence compartments and different lists of personnel with a "need to know" the information contained in that compartment. Covert operatives quickly learn to section off secrets in their own mind in order to avoid discussing a case with someone who has an equally high security clearance but who may not have access to the particular compartments implicated in that case, or even compartmentalized information within those compartments! The result is like a Mute button on conversation. If you can't be certain that your squad mate is "read into" the case you are working on, it's always best to just say nothing.

Working with Donner's squad taught me the opposite side of the investigations I would later work as a field operative. I collected and distilled data from the field, heard about how the ghost team following Pitts each day pursued the investigation, and saw in real time how the FBI agents frowned or cheered as surveillance logs came across the wire. I discovered the camaraderie to be found among a handpicked team of agents, each working toward a common goal, and I listened carefully to Donner's frequent warnings to say nothing about the case once we left the secret squad room in Buzzard Point. Over time, I became used to carrying secrets—though I was never fully comfortable. When friends asked me about my new job, I repelled any interest by saying the Department of Justice had hired me as a geopolitical analyst. Nobody felt the need to ask follow-up questions. It made it hard to capture the interest of a date, but it kept FBI-learned information safe.

On December 18, 1996, after I'd spent a few months on the investigation, we arrested Earl Pitts at the FBI Academy, where he worked at what was then called the Behavioral Science Unit—the unit tasked with applying behavioral and social sciences to investigative techniques, including profiling serial killers, countering violent extremism, and understanding psychopathology. In June 1997, after pleading guilty to conspiracy to commit espionage, Earl Pitts was sentenced to twenty-seven years in prison. I had long since left Donner's squad to finally attend the FBI Academy at Quantico, so I wasn't around for Pitts's lengthy debrief, when he mentioned that another FBI agent made him suspicious. Pitts suspected that agent might also be a spy. At the time, the FBI dismissed Pitts's concerns and chose not to follow up with the agent he'd named: an obscure computer expert named Robert Hanssen.

CHAPTER 3

LAY DOWN YOUR SWORD

Gene's blue Crown Victoria prowled away toward Pennsylvania Avenue and FBI headquarters. I watched him turn the corner and then stood for a few minutes in the cold. I had agreed to take a unique case based on very little information, and I still wasn't sure whether I had volunteered or been coerced. In a case where every scrap of knowledge was kept in a locked box inside other locked boxes, it seemed I had very few keys. Gene made sure I hadn't heard of Robert Hanssen, told me the FBI would investigate him for possible espionage, and got me to agree to share an office with him. I looked at my watch. It had taken Gene less than ten minutes to recruit me.

I would begin this case mostly blind, but after five years in the field as a ghost, I understood Gene's reasoning. Hanssen was a veteran agent, schooled in the tyranny of secrets. I was a pawn. And the less I knew about the case, the fewer details I could accidentally reveal.

Stomach tight and throat dry, I turned back toward my apartment. I'd come a long way since the Pitts case, I told myself. I had hunted spies and terrorists through parks and alleyways, offices and restaurants, shopping malls and nightclubs. I could manage an investigation at FBI headquarters.

I closed the door softly behind me. Before I could shrug off my coat, Juliana pressed a cup of coffee into my hands. The steaming mug warmed life into my frozen fingers. I sipped deeply, gathering my words.

Five years after my first polygraph test, I stood in front of my wife of less than a year and lied again. This would be the first lie I ever told her. It would also be far from the last.

"What did Gene want?" The slightest hint of a European accent rounded Juliana's question, made it beautiful.

"I just got promoted to a computer job at headquarters." The words came much too easily. I controlled my breath until the polygraph in my mind's eye stilled to only a straight blue line. "He said it will help me get to law school classes on time."

She brightened. "That's great! We should celebrate."

I tucked the Hanssen investigation away into a back part of my mind and compartmentalized. "Maybe my parents will have us over?"

That evening, Juliana and I were in our green Jeep Cherokee on the way to Kensington, Maryland. I tensed and bit my lip as she merged through the number four lane on the Capital Beltway to exit onto Connecticut Avenue. "Seriously, Eric!" She looked at me and rolled her eyes.

"Eyes on the road," I said. My white-knuckled grip on the dashboard matched my voice. "You'll wreck my car."

Her eyes flattened—hint of danger. "You mean *our* car."

"It won't be *our* car for long if you don't slow down."

Juliana sighed. "How do you ride with anyone at your job?"

"I'm usually the driver," I said. "Plus if someone else crashes an FBI car, I don't have to pay the bills."

"I won't crash."

Juliana knew that my aversion to riding as a passenger bordered on obsession. Much of my perhaps unhealthy conviction in my own driving ability stemmed from my FBI training. After graduating from the FBI's Tactical Emergency Vehicle

Operations course, and then refining that intense training against Russian spies on their way to drop sites, known terrorists priming their courage for an impending attack, and some of the best foreign operatives using the DC metro area as an espionage playground, I held every other driver to an impossible standard.

But Juliana had learned to drive from precise German instructors. When we first started dating, I'd asked her if she wanted to learn to drive stick. Desperate to impress her, I took her to a quiet alley and spent a good ten minutes lecturing her on using a clutch and shifting, finding the friction point with the left foot as the right slowly came off the gas, and shifting smoothly to avoid stalling the car. She listened to each explanation with the seriousness of an eager student and yielded to my multiple demonstrations of shifting into first. When I finally switched places with her, we barely had our seat belts on before she charged off like a drag racer seeing green lights. Juliana laughed away my shock and shifted from second to third so smoothly I had to watch to see it happen.

"Don't you know anything about Germany?" she said. "All the cars are stick shifts there."

Ever since that moment, Juliana has never missed an opportunity to insist she take the wheel. We could be like gasoline on fire that way sometimes. When both people want to be in control, neither can be happy until someone yields.

"I'm sorry," I said. "What's mine is yours."

"Better."

"Do you know the turn for my parents' house?"

She raised an eyebrow. "Yes, why?"

"I'm going to close my eyes and not look at the street."

I stepped out of the car onto my parents' driveway and looked up at the home where I'd spent six years before heading south in a packed Volkswagen van to attend college at Auburn University. The Victorian house had the kind of character that only comes from weathering countless families and numerous additions. But in 1987, during my freshman year of high school, it had been gutted by a fire. We had spent a year renting a tiny house a few blocks over while contractors repaired and remodeled this one. That lost year meant that the blue-painted shingles and solemn swing hanging under a decorative porch felt comfortable, but never quite like home to me.

My dad answered the front door and ushered us in with his usual bear hug. Dad grew up on a farm in Hartford County, Maryland, and built a lifetime's worth of muscle throwing hay bales into the back of tractor-pulled carts. He'd joined the Navy not only to follow a family tradition but also to escape the horrible hay fever that he'd generously passed on to me—there aren't many hay fields in submarines.

We found my mother in the kitchen, stirring a pot of pasta sauce. The smells of garden tomatoes, mushrooms, and fresh basil mingling with her secret ingredient, a cup of wine, finally made me feel at home. The kitchen had always been my mother's favorite part of the house, which may have had something to do with the house she grew up in, a split-level town house in Jamaica, Queens. When I say split-level, I mean that the family who lived upstairs walked through my mother's kitchen to leave through the front door. Mom had escaped those cramped circumstances by attending Hunter College in Manhattan and becoming a nurse. This evening, my mother's dark eyes flashed with intrigue. "Tell me about your promotion."

I frowned. The twinge in my stomach had nothing to do with my itch to grab a bowl and race to the kitchen table. I hated the thought of lying to my mother. My parents knew I worked for the FBI, but I had never told them about the ghosts.

"It's a computer job," I said, forcing the words out. "I'll be working in a new division, but they haven't told me all the details yet."

My father brandished a bottle of wine. "You don't tell us much about what you did before, so . . ." The cork came away with a pop. "Any excuse to celebrate!"

Juliana helped my mother smother bowls of pasta in sauce. "For once, Eric is being modest," she said. "His boss came by our house personally to tell him about the promotion." She paused for effect. "On a Sunday."

Dad looked up from where he filled our wineglasses. "Couldn't wait until Monday?"

I took two bowls from Juliana and avoided her eyes. I could already feel the lies piling up, so I simply shrugged. I could only think back to my first polygraph exam and how, once again, I was lying to someone who loved me.

"How is law school?" My mom changed the subject.

Speaking about my legal studies placed me on solid ground. I hadn't followed my father's footsteps into a navy career, but I had followed him into a second family tradition in the practice of law. After three years ghosting targets, I realized that if I wanted to move up within the FBI, I would need an advanced degree. I dreamed of graduating from George Washington University Law School and applying to the Special Agents Program, or trading in my disguise kit for a position at the Justice Department. I had started law school at night uncertain about where exactly it would take me, but I'd always felt drawn to the sanctuary of rules and laws. I hoped attending law school would allow me to continue to serve my country, but as the person calling the plays rather than the one in the field.

"The new job will help," I said. "I'll be working a nine-to-five desk at headquarters, so no more missed classes when I have to work nights."

We migrated to the table and took our seats. Out of the corner of my eye, I watched my mother's laborious walk from stove to table and ground my teeth as she fell more than sat into her chair. My parents had first told me about her Parkinson's disease in a tearful phone call during my third year at Auburn University. Years later, the disease had progressed enough to slur her speech and make walking more difficult. It also affected her facial expressions. My temperamental mother, who could switch from an angry shout to a beatific smile in a second, now struggled to lift her cheeks.

"Do you have a title for this new job?" Dad asked.

"Not yet." I took a sip of wine. Avoided eye contact. "They really haven't told me anything."

"Do you have time for it?" Dad refreshed half-full wineglasses. "You've got a lot on your plate."

My father's understatement sent a needless shot of adrenaline through me. A few words shouldn't kick me into fight or flight, but when your life is an arena, it's hard to lay down your sword. Each day felt more and more about surviving to the next, not living the one before me. Survival didn't mean patience with those I loved, or time for friends or family. Nor did it mean careless moments free of the pressing concerns that orbited me. I wanted to build on my new marriage, not scour law books late at night, chase spies during the day, and worry about my mother's decline during the few hours I should be sleeping. Even before the Hanssen investigation swept apart the house of cards I'd built of my life, I'd already set it on fire.

My parents exchanged a look. Finally my mother shrugged in that very Italian way that means: *Whattaya gonna do?*

Dad raised his glass. "To Eric and Juliana. New beginnings and new opportunities."

I made sure to meet Juliana's eyes as we clinked glasses—one of her few superstitions. "*Prost.*"

We said our goodbyes, and Juliana graciously let me drive home. We opened the door into our tiny combination kitchen/living room. As tight a squeeze as it was, I felt more at home there than in all my years in Maryland. Juliana and I had hung photos from our shared lives in clever spaces. The old couch we'd inherited from my uncle Ralph proudly wore a slipcover Juliana had sewed during the long, boring month she spent waiting for her student visa. A television wobbled precariously on top of a corner cabinet that we'd picked out together from IKEA and assembled, cursing playfully as we followed the complex instructions. Our short lives together so far surrounded us with promise. Better days would come.

As soon as we walked in the door, we heard an elderly voice echoing from upstairs: "Hello! Hello!"

We both glanced at the ceiling and laughed. We'd heard the Hello Lady since we moved in, night after night for about an hour. The first time we had heard the repeated greeting, we had tried to answer back. If the woman in the apartment above us heard, she gave no sign. Instead, she—or someone, anyway—would continue saying hello in a singsong voice over and over. It was the great mystery of 626 E Street.

Juliana grinned. "It has to be a bird."

"Or she's just talking to herself."

"It's a bird." Juliana pulled me into an embrace. "I just know."

I glanced at the old clock that squatted on the mantel of our non-functioning fireplace. "At least she's consistent. Every night at eight p.m. on the dot."

"Every place has a story."

I looked around us. Thought of my parents' home. "Do you ever want more than this?"

"More than what?" Juliana teased.

"It's cold and drafty. The heater barely works. We had to save for months to buy the TV. . . ."

She drew back just enough for me to see her face. Her green eyes, flecked with gold, sparkled. "My mom had a saying, something she told my dad when they were first married and moved into my grandfather's house together. Mom didn't even speak German. She had to learn my father's language before they could have a conversation." She smiled. "We will just live on love and air."

"Air doesn't pay the bills."

"Hello. Hello." Juliana breathed in my ear until I finally smiled. Then she pulled me back through another tiny hallway and through the door to our bedroom.

"Hello yourself."

CHAPTER 4

MOUSETRAP

December 20, 2000—Wednesday

I followed Gene through the maze of FBI headquarters. Gray hallway yielded to gray hallway, illuminated by fluorescent lights and the occasional hint of sunlight through an open office door. Multicolored strips—like hieroglyphics—on the walls hinted at directions to cryptic locations. I couldn't break the code and was soon lost, trailing Gene like a faithful hound.

Before that moment, I had only set foot in headquarters once, when I was in training at Quantico. Many of the future ghosts in my class had never toured the nation's capital and had declared me tour guide over a free weekend. After exploring monuments and museums, we had stopped in FBI HQ to raid the gift shop. Christmas was right around the corner, and my little brothers delighted in wearing official FBI gear. This visit had none of the laughter and camaraderie of my former one. Instead, I marched at a sober pace toward a meeting that could make or break my career.

"Through here," Gene said. "Be polite. Make me proud."

Gene ushered me through an office of administrative workstations. A smartly dressed woman in her thirties looked up from her monitor as Gene approached, scrutinized him, and then waved us past. She barely glanced at me before returning to her work.

I looked past Gene to the door at the far side of the room,

and my heart kicked up a notch. The placard beside the door read ASSISTANT DIRECTOR BOB DIES.

I quietly thanked Juliana. Over the New Year's holiday, she had insisted that we buy a new suit for my new job. After a few hours in Macy's, we'd emerged with a navy-blue suit, two ties, and a few trim white shirts that didn't require me to twist in front of a mirror to stuff away the excess cloth. As a ghost, you have to be able to blend into any situation, and my standard outfit of light pants with useful cargo pockets and a collared shirt fit most of them. I could walk unnoticed across a college campus; transform myself into a Washington, DC, tourist; and stroll into the majority of restaurants, bars, shops, and malls without anyone turning an eye. Sometimes I would exchange trousers for biker shorts and a backpack; in the years before the terrorist actions of September 11, bike messengers could walk into any building. Very rarely would I shrug into my only suit in order to chase a target into an elegant restaurant or stodgy office building. Before Juliana took me to Macy's, that suit was the same black one I wore to funerals.

She had also turned her nose up at my battered but highly trusted backpack. I had cut a pinhole in the front pocket to hide a small concealment camera, and if you looked closely, you could see tiny marks on the shoulder straps that allowed me to hide radio wires. Juliana argued that the backpack wasn't professional and had insisted I buy a shiny leather briefcase. We'd compromised on a black-and-gray Timberland messenger bag that now hung off my shoulder. While I didn't wear a suit and tie as effortlessly as Gene, I felt confident that I at least wouldn't embarrass myself in front of the assistant director.

I had stuffed a few items into the messenger bag: a legal pad and pen to take notes, my FBI credentials that told others in law enforcement whom I worked for and the golden badge that proved it, and a letter that Gene had handed me at the field office to make my part in the Hanssen investigation official. The letter had come from Assistant Director Dies's office and had assigned me to his office for temporary duty (TDY, in FBI-speak) of one year. I would report directly to Section Chief Richard Garcia and would be assigned to the Information Assurance/Security Team. The carefully drafted letter created my cover for the assignment to Hanssen:

> AD Dies requested Investigative Specialist O'Neill be TDY'd to FBIHQ IRD Information Assurance/Security Team (IAST) based on O'Neill's computer expertise and familiarity with National Security Division and counterintelligence matters as they relate to computer hardware, software, and systems. AD Dies also noted his desire for a field office perspective to the envisioned work of the IAST.

Reading the TDY letter, I could almost believe that the FBI had truly promoted me. To fool Hanssen, I'd have to sell the story to everyone, including myself.

"Speak little, nod in the right places," Gene said. Then he opened the door.

AD Dies looked up from his desk and motioned for us to take a seat. I eased into a comfortable leather chair and resisted the urge to sink backward. The assistant director had his shirt-sleeves rolled up and looked slightly frazzled behind the array of papers spread across his desk. He swiped a pair of wireframe glasses from his face and rubbed his eyes.

"Assistant Director Dies, sir." Gene's voice took on a formal tone I hadn't heard before. "This is IS O'Neill."

An open IBM ThinkPad to one side of the desk drew my envy. The model was top of the line, complete with a track pad and the little nub mouse embedded in the keyboard that everyone called an eraser. Totally out of bounds for the FBI rank and file, but entirely appropriate for a man with Dies's pedigree.

After thirty years at IBM, where he'd last served as a vice president and general manager for the company's network and personal computer division, Dies had been about to retire when FBI Director Louis Freeh convinced him to take on what he called "the toughest job in the FBI today." Dies would lead the FBI's Information Research Division (IRD) as an assistant director and member of the director's senior staff.

In the late 1990s, the newly interconnected world had left the FBI behind. IRD was responsible for drafting a modernization plan that would wake the FBI up to the new networked reality. Under Dies's leadership, IRD would upgrade computer systems and networks and invest in new hardware and software platforms that would enhance the FBI's mission. The new assistant director had a steep hill to climb.

Dies caught me staring at his laptop. "I'd like one of those on the desk of every agent," he said.

I glanced at Gene, but he kept his expression neutral. Was this a test? "They would be just as useful in the field, sir," I said.

The assistant director slid his glasses back over his eyes and looked at me over folded hands. "I heard about your computer program."

It wasn't a question. I followed Gene's instructions and kept silent despite the thrill that squared my shoulders. Dies sifted through a few sheets of paper. "Your squad has some of the latest computer systems and even a few laptops." He looked at Gene. "This is left over from a pilot program?"

"The idea was to allow specialists to upload surveillance logs directly into a database that would then coordinate the information." Gene paused. "IS O'Neill could explain this better. He wrote the program."

I had organized and led the effort to computerize our squad ahead of most of the FBI, even to the point of sending ghost teams out with laptops. Lengthy periods of downtime during molasses-paced surveillance operations leave a lot of time to type up a log. The ghost with log duty could then upload the electronic file directly into the target database on the same day as the surveillance. Prior to computerization, it might be days before a ghost would cycle out of the field for an administra-

tive day of typing up logs, training, car and equipment mainte-
nance, weightlifting, and practical jokes played on other teams.

Dies looked at me. I tried not to squirm. "I . . . sir . . . I had
the idea after following Russians. . . ." I looked at Gene. Could
I say any of this? He nodded.

"Russians usually work based on a series of points in time.
They prearrange their signals and dead drops and whatever
ahead of time so that they rarely have to communicate in person or over the phone with an asset." I wished I could use a
whiteboard, but Dies's stare made me go on. "I got the idea that
if we catalog all those dates over time, we would see a pattern."

Dies looked at Gene.

"We found a pattern, all right," Gene said.

"And you wrote this in wha?" Dies said. "C++?"

I took a breath. "Actually, Microsoft Access."

"Access!" Dies sat back.

You could cook an egg on my face. My interest in computer
systems began in 1986 when my mother bought our first Apple
IIGS out of the first proceeds from a catering company she
started. I taught myself rudimentary programming so that I
could modify video games and soon graduated to building my
own computer systems and then to challenging my newfound
knowledge by testing security as I explored the nascent World
Wide Web. I could program, but I didn't have time or funding
to create a database from scratch for the FBI. "We didn't have a
budget, and Microsoft Office was already installed on the desktop Gene assigned me. Sir, I used what I had in front of me.
Also, I'm used to using a mouse. I wanted to design something
that didn't look left over from the 1970s."

Dies laughed, but I could hear the underlying morbidity in
the mirth. I had touched on a sore spot for the FBI. After the
turn of the twenty-first century, the FBI's primary computer
program was an obsolete, mainframe-based program called the
Automated Case System. Because none of the FBI computers
had enough horsepower to run a distributed program like ACS,

the information resided on a powerful mainframe computer that the desktop in a squad office would connect to in order to access case information. To upload a single document into ACS, an agent had to traverse a dozen green screens that looked like they would fit right into the movie *War Games*. The system was incompatible with Microsoft Windows OS, which was already ubiquitous in the civilian world. And as slow and complicated as it was to use ACS, it was still ultimately just a filing system used to direct legions of assistants and clerks to hunt down paper files. In a nutshell, everyone hated it.

My system uploaded all our investigative logs into a Microsoft database that allowed the user to perform keyword searches over time and dates, either specific moments or ranges of them. It also allowed a user to instantly retrieve any surveillance log in Word format. No more hunting down old information in dusty file cabinets. You could keyword-search a Russian intelligence officer by name and see how many times ghosts had followed him over the past year to a certain telephone pole that we knew served as a Russian signal site. If the system showed that he had passed that signal site at three o'clock every second Tuesday of the month for a year, you could plan to set up ahead of him the next month and increase the odds of breaking a major case.

Of course, Dies didn't know that I didn't have entirely altruistic reasons for creating the database. I needed a way to spend more time at law school and less time out on the street missing class. I proposed the program to my supervisory special agent with the caveat that I'd code during the day on weeks when my team had overnight operations.

The idea had come to me when I'd started law school and began using Westlaw and LexisNexis, databases that served as searchable, cross-indexed law libraries. If every lawyer in the United States could call up every case related to the one they were working on with just a few mouse clicks, why couldn't the FBI do the same? The FBI should have come up with the idea of approaching major systems designers to develop a Westlaw or Lexis for the bureau. Instead they had an investigative specialist in his mid-twenties coding modules in Access during rare days in the office and on nights and weekends. But the fact that my database worked got me noticed by the powers that be.

"Don't worry, Eric," Dies said. "We are going to change everything." He reached across the desk to shake my hand. "Welcome to the team."

A smile finally ghosted Gene's face.

Once we were back out in the hall and safe from other ears, I asked Gene whether Dies knew about the Hanssen investigation. "That's need-to-know," Gene answered. "You don't have a need to know."

Gene led me back through the halls filled with the noisy chatter of FBI employees. We rode an elevator up two floors to the ninth and stepped out into a clinical hallway of white walls and drop ceilings striped with bright, cased fluorescent lights. Doors framed in dark wood stood an even-spaced sentry until the hall ended in a sharp left turn. Just to the right of the elevators, the bathrooms faced each other inside an alcove divided by a water fountain.

Gene looked over and chuckled. "What's the first rule of surveillance?"

"Never inspect a bathroom, and never pass one by."

He slapped me on the back. "Well done! Who told you that?"

"Tom Reilly. While we worked the Earl Pitts case." Tom was a counterintelligence agent, years my senior, who had taken me under his wing. One afternoon while rushing after Pitts, Tom had stopped us both by a public restroom. I'd told him to go ahead, I didn't feel the need, but he'd lectured me about opportunity. "You'll find yourself trapped in a car chasing a target though streets with no end and that's when the need will strike," Tom had said. "So when you have downtime, always hit the head. And when you're in there, don't inspect: get in, do your business, and get out quick before your target moves again."

In all my years as an undercover operative, that advice had been the most important.

"Tom's a good guy," Gene said. "Here's another."

Gene led me through an open door into an office that looked pleasantly out of place in the otherwise drab headquarters. A glass-fronted bookcase of polished wood held thick volumes related to operations and investigations. A massive executive desk dominated one side of the carpeted room. A comfortable couch that matched the voluminous desk chair relaxed along the opposite wall. The walls and shelves were decorated with baseball memorabilia, along with numerous awards and plaques in both English and Spanish.

"Eric, meet Rich Garcia."

Garcia's exuberant smile under his burly mustache and thick glasses made the corner of my mouth tick up. We shook hands. "Anything you need," Garcia said, "I'm here. Just right down the hall."

I looked at Gene.

"Rich is in the know," Gene confirmed. "As far as you are concerned, he's the only person at headquarters that knows about the investigation."

Richard Garcia's FBI career had followed a unique trajectory. He had joined the FBI out of the Dallas Police Department and had continued to serve as a Dallas FBI agent until an assignment in San Juan, Puerto Rico, landed him a spot in Miami and then a position at FBI headquarters supervising a Colombian/South American Drug Traffickers Unit. Years later he would return to Texas as assistant special agent in charge of the FBI's El Paso office before finally returning to headquarters as section chief in charge of information technology operations.

"All the cameras you see in the halls, the security systems, the phone systems, and every lock on every door. That's all out of my section," Garcia explained. "We are installing tech in the office to monitor that bastard."

"Got it," I said. But I didn't.

"I'm taking him to the room," Gene said.

Garcia glanced at the unfinished work on his desk. "Kate's there. I'll be along later."

I hiked up my shoulder bag and remembered that the letter Gene had shown me hadn't just TDY'd me to HQ; it had also technically placed me under Garcia's supervision. I realized I knew next to nothing about this assignment. Only that the FBI somehow expected me to help catch a spy.

"O'Neill." Garcia stopped me before I could follow Gene from the room. "If it ever gets too hot in there, if you need help: I'm right down the hall."

"Thank you, sir." I could tell he was speaking in earnest, but I couldn't decide whether his words comforted me or made me more apprehensive.

"The room is a few doors down," Gene said. For once we didn't have to thread a maze of featureless corridors broken only by red and blue color-coded markers. Gene led me a short way down an empty hallway toward the rolling whine of drills and dull thumps of hammers.

"The room?"

Gene escorted me through a doorway framed in black steel. A massive door hung open on heavy hinges. I spotted holes in the top and bottom rails where bolts would secure the door to its frame. A combination dial bulged above a latch that I could fit both my hands on. A lonely placard displayed the room number in red, blue, and black: 9930.

"On paper, you are TDY'd to headquarters and to Garcia's desk," Gene said. "Covertly, you're assigned to the WFO team investigating Hanssen." Gene stopped me. "This is important. As far as you are concerned, no one knows about this case. Mum's the word. Not me, not your wife or grandma. Not even Garcia. You discuss this case with only one person. Eric, meet Special Agent Kate Alleman."

Special Agent Alleman had worked in army intelligence before coming over to the civilian side, and she moved with the grace of someone familiar with the track and the weight room. Streaks of blond shot through her short brown hair. Though her smile needed little prompting to break through, I could tell there was steel within her. I didn't yet know it, but that fortitude would guide me like an evening star.

Kate shook my hand and pulled me into Room 9930. This was where I would be working one on one, side by side, with Robert Hanssen. I still had no idea who Hanssen was, what he was suspected of doing, or what kind of dirt I was expected to find, and Kate wasn't about to tell me. She dodged my questions and broadly explained the crux of the situation: after a career of rattling the wrong cages, never shy about letting his superiors know he thought them foolish or incompetent, Hanssen had been banished to an obscure desk job at the State Department. (I was also told he'd had a dispute with a subordinate that involved him screaming, and ended with her sprawled on the floor.) This was because the government rarely fires an employee, even for cause. Instead, the FBI shuffles its unwanted souls to administrative hell, where they're put out to pasture, left to boredom or advancement Siberia until they quit or retire. Which was exactly our problem: Hanssen was about to hit mandatory retirement in just a couple of months.

You might think that the FBI would wish the suspected spy good riddance, but then you wouldn't understand the spy game. The only way a spy hunter could possibly catch Hanssen in an act of espionage was to keep him working at the bureau—meaning the FBI needed to woo Hanssen back from his cushy, if boring, job at State. They needed to coax him back into the fold in a way that would mend his fractured ego, give him access to juicy information, and encourage him to spy. And they needed to do all that without tipping him off that he was walking into a mousetrap. Much like the way Donner's squad operated during the Earl Pitts case, the squad investigating Hanssen wanted to slowly build a case. A key difference was that no FBI agents would false-flag Hanssen. We wanted him to spy for the actual Russians.

To accomplish this impossible task, the powers that be decided to give Hanssen his dream job. He'd spent years complaining that the FBI's systems were vulnerable to outside hackers and inside spies, and the FBI had spent years ignoring his concerns. Now, at the twilight of his career, they were capitulating. Imagine Hanssen's surprise when the FBI told him not only that he would be returning to headquarters to start a new squad to protect the FBI from computer espionage but also that the new role included a promotion to executive service. Hanssen would make more money and get the fancy office he had spent twenty-five years dreaming about. The deal was too good to pass up—but also too good to be true.

Contractors had split Room 9930 into a main office for Hanssen and a second, larger squad room for me. Hanssen would have an executive desk and a credenza, a coatrack, and a TV stand—all standard issue for an agent in executive service—as well as a safe rated for special compartmentalized information (SCI). My office would contain a few more modest desks, a separate computer station for accessing the Internet, and a copier. The extra desks were just for show. Hanssen would only ever have a staff of one.

In the meantime, however, workers had been busy gutting the room that Kate walked me into. Wires slithered from unfinished walls pocked with holes. Uninstalled equipment waited on top of every flat surface. I couldn't identify half of it. The FBI had classified the room as a sensitive compartmented information facility (SCIF—pronounced "skiff"). This meant that within 9930, Hanssen and I could analyze and access information classified as top secret/SCI. It also meant that 9930 was in an interior office without windows, that technicians had soundproofed the walls and vents, and that they'd installed a door that belonged on an Egyptian pharaoh's tomb. There were hidden cameras and surveillance equipment all across the room.

"If you have all these cameras, what do you need me for?" I asked.

I received the first of many trademark Kate grins. Somewhere between supportive and condescending, it had a way of making you reach back inside yourself to answer a question you'd just asked.

"You never rely on technology alone," Kate said. "The most important wins come from people. Not machines. We can't see everything. That's your job. Watch and listen."

I nodded, chewing over the question that had needled me since Gene pulled me out of bed: Out of everyone in the bureau, why had the agents selected me for this role? At age twenty-six, I could dress up to play the part of a seasoned corporate professional, but I could also stroll through a high school without attracting a second glance. As a ghost, I could *21 Jump Street* across a college campus, but since meeting Juliana, I'd been shouldered into second-string cases. This feeling drove me to push the boundaries: selecting choke points ahead of targets in shadowed alleys, hanging off the edge of rooftops to find the perfect camera angle, spending nights and weekends developing a target-tracking database to make the entire squad more efficient. All these things lent me a certain reputation, but they didn't change the fact that, according to the training manuals, I was the wrong person to take on what appeared to be a high-level suspected spy. But sometimes in the spy game a perceived disadvantage can become an asset. Maybe an older, more seasoned and well-trained agent couldn't do the job that I could.

"Any tips for me?" I asked.

"Just be yourself," Kate answered.

I tried to swallow, but the sound of the ticking clock made my mouth go dry. It was January, and Hanssen's twenty-five-year retirement was coming up in April. I didn't have much in the way of information, but I did know I only had a few months to help catch a suspected spy.

CHAPTER 5

THE WEAKEST LINK

January 16, 2001—Tuesday

The chilly January morning layered Washington, DC, in stark grays. Black streets cut precise paths past stone buildings and forgotten monuments, everything solid and immobile under the heavy sky. The air frosted ahead of my labored breath. I'd jogged up the many escalator steps emerging from the Archives–Navy Memorial Metro station and then walked with purpose toward the sandstone-colored temple that was the FBI Building. Now my hurry had stalled against the weight of a single moment. Kate had advised me to "be myself." How could I be myself when I felt like an actor playing my part in a movie?

It had taken the going-away party with my ghost squad for me to appreciate how strictly the FBI had compartmentalized the Hanssen investigation. Officially, only a handful of my fellow ghosts tasked with surveilling Hanssen knew why the FBI had transferred me to headquarters. The rest of the Special Surveillance Group (SSG) in WFO believed the same lie I had told Juliana: I had accepted a computer-security job. I knew that the teams shadowing Hanssen's every step would never tell. The SSG is the most highly compartmentalized group in the FBI. Ghosts learn to say nothing about the work they accomplish for fear that an errant word might reach the wrong ear. The Roman poet Juvenal wrote in his *Satires* "*Quis custodiet ipsos custodies?*" The Latin question literally means "Who will guard the guards themselves?" but is more commonly translated as "Who will watch the watchers?" Among the secret hallways of the SSG, we silently watched one another.

Our silence with respect to classified matters did not stifle the usual banter and interpersonal drama that blossoms within a close-knit team. We could care about one another while burying our secrets. And so, a few days before I stood in front of FBI headquarters on that cold January morning, the assortment of oddballs and jokers that I trusted to have my back each day we chased spies and terrorists through the DC streets celebrated my move to the Big House.

Friends circulated flyers for "Eric O'Neill's Luncheon" in our office. We descended on a buffet at Charlie Chiang's in Shirlington, Virginia, and clinked beer glasses in a toast to my future as an FBI HQ computer nerd. I smiled along, but secretly wondered how many of my fellows knew what my actual role would be and were laughing inwardly as they watched me pretend graciousness. How many would later learn that the "promotion" was a smokescreen for the FBI's grandest spy-hunting operation? Would they see the deception as another secret tucked into one of many compartments? Or would they feel that I had cheated them out of a $13 lunch?

I'd had the same sick feeling over New Year's. Juliana and I rang in the first moments of 2001 with our best friends Mike and Vivian under fireworks in Orlando, Florida. I had known Mike since we shared a desk in Ms. Fredrickson's first-grade class at the Saint Jane Frances de Chantal elementary school in Bethesda, Maryland, and I was overjoyed when his long-time girlfriend Viv started becoming close to Juliana. Juliana eventually asked Viv to be her maid of honor at our wedding. We were excited to celebrate the holiday together, and we'd planned a weekend of amusement parks, great restaurants, and maybe a little drinking to excess. But that was all before Gene had shown up in front of 626 E Street. During a New Year's Eve party, I stood and listened as my oldest friend and my very new wife applauded my new job. Maybe it was the Champagne that brought a smile to my face at my pal's flowery words. Or maybe the lies that now continually crossed my lips were starting to flow more easily. Neither possibility sat well with me.

The J. Edgar Hoover Building, named for the first director of the FBI, is a nearly 3-million-square-foot Brutalist monstrosity that squats on Pennsylvania Avenue a stone's throw from the Capitol Building. The lopsided structure is actually two buildings of different heights connected by two wings that surround an interior trapezoid-shaped courtyard. Three of its floors plus a parking garage are completely underground. It was the sort of building that might swallow a person up just for the crime of walking inside.

I adjusted my shoulder bag and turned up the collar of my new overcoat against the cold. My single act of rebellion against the stodgy dress that overwhelmed the hallowed halls of the FBI was to replace the small lapel clip on my FBI Secure Access Control System key card, known as a SACS badge, with a green Caffrey's Irish Ale lanyard I'd won at bar trivia. Small shamrocks traced the thick cord like a little luck around my neck. I wasn't a special agent, and no one would ever confuse me for James Bond, but I'd done my damnedest to look the part.

I squared my shoulders, plastered a cocky grin over my chattering teeth, and strode to the entrance off Ninth Street with the purpose of someone intent on changing the world. I showed my SACS badge to the bored FBI security officer at the security desk. He waved me by without a second glance. I belonged here. I could do this!

I was lost.

My bravado eloped with my courage and defected. I coughed back an irrational panic. The elevator topped out at the eighth floor of the sprawling FBI HQ complex. I followed the echo of my steps down a quiet hallway, looking for an upward stairwell. Any ghost with an ounce of training would find me suspicious. Tentative movements, checking my watch every few minutes,

loosening my tie as my breath came hoarse and stubborn, fur-
tive glances around corners and upward toward security cameras. I cringed at the thought of arriving late for my first day
on the job. If I couldn't even find the ninth floor in my own
headquarters building, when I'd already been there once before with Gene, how was I supposed to catch a spy?

I backtracked to the elevator and down to the security guard.
The affable FBI police officer could have tried harder to hide
his laughter as he explained the lay of the land. I'd spent my
career learning to blend into every situation. Now I felt like a
naked guy trying to hide behind a planter in the middle of a
crowded shopping mall. I was a stupid kid in a big-person suit
with a beer lanyard around my neck.

The two-tower design of FBI HQ meant that elevators on
the Pennsylvania Avenue side only went up eight floors. I would
have to either take the elevator back to the sixth floor and
thread the labyrinth or walk around the outside of the building to the entrance on E Street.

I chose the second option and headed out the door I'd come
in. Without thinking, I walked a few steps toward the Metro
before wrestling my feet around. Despite my misgivings, I had
a job to accomplish. I thought about what my parents would say
if they saw me wandering away from my duty.

As a child, I never dreamed of joining the FBI. Although I've
always loved Bond movies, my earliest ambitions aimed far away
from Earth's problems. I was NASA-bound.

The logical step toward astronautics was to join the military,
at least in my family. My father's father served as a navy gun-
nery officer in the Pacific; I grew up with childhood fantasies of
him leaning back into a deck cannon and personally shooting
kamikazes out of the sky. As a nurse, my mother started the first
maternity ward at the naval hospital in Charleston, South Caro-
lina. And my father was an Annapolis graduate handpicked by
Admiral Rickover to serve as one of the first nuclear submarine
officers in the Navy.

Dad made it back to shore a day before my birth, and thereafter traded his commission for a berth at Yale Law School. My mother worked at the hospital while my father studied. While Mom earned our family bread and put my father through law school, Dad spent quiet afternoons reading me stories in our wicker rocking chair.

After graduating at the top of his class, my father took an energy-litigation job with a DC law firm. My mother quit medicine to raise four sons, but also ran her own business between school pickups, homework, and all the various sports four kids can pursue. She never slowed down until Parkinson's disease slammed the brakes on her vitality, and even then she soldiered on as long as possible.

My family prizes achievement, duty, and hard work. An O'Neill never quits.

I poured myself into honors mathematics at Gonzaga High School, only steps from the Capitol Building, spent weekends learning to fly a Cessna 172 at Montgomery Air Field, and even spent a summer at Space Camp in Huntsville, Alabama. When the Naval Academy deferred my acceptance for a year, I chose Auburn University for its elite Aerospace Engineering curriculum instead of opting for a Navy preparatory school. I would attend Auburn, returning to my Southern roots for a year, and then start over at the Naval Academy as a midshipman, where I'd have an engineering edge on the rest of my class.

But a year in engineering and the ROTC didn't invigorate me like I thought it would. I still loved math, but I found myself drawn away from the science of numbers and toward the science of the mind. I walked onto the Auburn lacrosse team and within a year started as a face-off midfielder. I met a girl from Georgia and thought I could stop searching for happiness. Those dreams of flying for the Navy on my way to space took a backseat to new dreams and an equal set of challenges.

One quiet Sunday, perched on an uncomfortable Victorian settee in my mother's formal living room, I told my parents that I had decided to stay at Auburn and forgo our shared dreams of a Navy commission. I would leave engineering for psychology, political science, and law. I wanted to understand the motivations behind a person's decisions more than I wanted to calculate the distances between stars.

My mother cried quietly, but not out of anger. To my surprise, instead of disowning me, my father smiled away a touch of disappointment and told me that I had to follow my own path. If my decision to walk away from the Navy was not due to personal failure, but because I saw a different opportunity, my parents would support me.

I graduated from Auburn University with honors and with a new plan. My degrees in psychology and political science made me set my sights on a legal career, but I wanted at least a year of experience in the outside world before diving back into academia. I settled in as an economic consultant, organizing numbers in databases to tell litigators how much they could sue for. My life became a relentless series of Excel spreadsheets and long flights. Within a few months, I knew I'd fallen off my path.

A year to the day after I'd started, I walked into my boss's office and quit my consulting job. My Navy dreams had passed me by, but I could still serve my country. I filled out index cards and mailed them to every alphabet agency I could find in the phonebook. The FBI, NSA, Secret Service, and DEA all sent back thick applications that I fed into my old typewriter. (The CIA never responded. Their loss.)

I decided to focus my efforts on the FBI and the DEA. In the early '90s, you had to be at least twenty-five to become an FBI special agent, but my application had caught the attention of the SSG. The DEA didn't care if I was twenty-two or thirty, as long as I met its rigorous physical standards, had the mental discipline to know when to shoot, and could keep calm under fire. Both the FBI and DEA house their training academies on the US Marine base in Quantico, Virginia. I decided to choose whichever agency gave me a berth at Quantico first.

The FBI called a day before the DEA. I've never heard a person curse as colorfully as the DEA recruiter when I told him I'd already joined the FBI, but I smiled as I hung up the phone. I would serve my country. In that service, I would cast off regret and find my way back to my path. It was a big leap, but knew I'd chosen correctly.

Now, standing in front of FBI HQ, I called on that feeling of purpose again. The bureau had called me to serve. Quitting wasn't an option.

I stepped out of a different elevator onto a polished hallway I recognized. Bathrooms to my right and a stairwell to my left. I passed four offices on my left, including Rich Garcia's, and a secretary station and file room on my right, then a few steps farther to Room 9930.

The plaque to the right of the door read IA/ST (Information Assurance/Security Team), with the numbers 9930 set in white on blue, red, and black strips. Below it, a white keypad stared back at me with a single red LED, now dark. Grateful that Kate had taken me for a dry run, I ignored my shaking hands and passed my SACS badge over the red LED, bringing the eye to life. I then punched a code that Kate had made me memorize into a small keypad and examined the heavy safe combination dial. Someone had already entered the combination and unlocked the deadbolts. I fished in my pocket for a key and inserted it into the doorknob. The lock clicked, and a loud beep announced my entrance into the SCIF. The lights in the main room were already on, and I could hear shuffling coming from the office.

Hanssen didn't come out, so I crossed the room and hovered before his open office door. My new supervisor was tall and lanky in an off-the-rack navy suit over a crisp white shirt. He wore a red tie that I would come to know well; he'd change it once in two months. I placed him in his late fifties, more than twice my age.

Hanssen had left his overhead lights off. A desk lamp cast

more shadows than light across the stark space. The television on the other side of the room glowed with a real-time feed of Pennsylvania Avenue as seen from a rooftop camera.

When Hanssen stood up, I saw that he had three or four inches on me. As he came around the desk, the keys in his pocket jingled. He had a slight limp that made each step a lurch. His dour expression bore down with a physical weight, and I could see why he'd received the nicknames "Dr. Death" and "The Mortician" around the FBI.

I reached out a hand. "Bob Hanssen? Hello, I'm—"

He held up one long-fingered hand. "You can call me sir, or boss."

A bead of sweat dripped down my back. I held on to my mask and shook hands with Hanssen. "Okay, boss," I said.

"Get yourself situated at your desk. I'm busy right now. We'll talk soon."

I retreated to my brightly lit desk and blinked as my eyes adjusted back from the gloom. An old IBM desktop squatted beside an ancient monitor. I frowned at a system so obsolete the FBI couldn't donate it to charity. The system I'd built on my home workbench could run circles around this dusty monster, something I'd told the FBI on a number of occasions. How could we assure information if our data crept through machines that couldn't even run outdated security software?

The FBI's mission is to protect the American people and uphold the Constitution of the United States. The bureau traditionally accomplished this mission by investigating crime and protecting the nation against foreign and domestic spies and terrorists. In the past, FBI agents would rattle doorknobs and pound the pavement, conduct elaborate sting operations, and orchestrate raids on a bounty of paper files seized from potential criminals and spies. Trained analysts sifted through that information, essentially functioning as human data processors. They relied on decades of experience to identify the patterns and find the evidence that broke cases, assured successful prosecutions, and carved the FBI's legacy into the stone of history.

Somehow along the way, however, technology left the FBI behind. Five years before I first entered Room 9930, when I was manipulating Excel spreadsheets for the consulting company that had driven me to the bureau in the first place, the civilian world had already embraced digital data over paper. When I first joined the SSG, I was shocked to witness analysts arguing over piles of physical surveillance logs as they attempted to predict a target's next location. It boggled my mind that the FBI took days to accomplish what a simple database could manage in a search that took less than a second.

In July 2001, Assistant Director Dies would testify before Congress that the FBI was suffering from a lack of modernization. Criminals across the world were able to dodge the FBI's long arm by ensuring that their technological savvy stayed one step ahead of law enforcement. The FBI needed to up its game.

One look at the aged IBM beside my desk told me we were losing the battle. In the year 2000, more than 13,000 FBI desktops were four to eight years old and couldn't run the most basic software that American teenagers had been enjoying for years. FBI agents spent hours tapping through screens of information using complex keystrokes. Few of them would know what to do with a mouse even if you could install one.

Civilian businesses and most neighborhoods had graduated to DSL connectivity, but smaller FBI offices and field sites connected to the FBI's internal network at speeds equivalent to a 56KB modem. The minimalist FBI databases couldn't store detailed investigative information like photographs or graphical and tabular data. Forget calling up a video of a crime scene—or of a spy setting a signal or approaching a drop site. Dies testified that "fundamentally, at the dawn of the twenty-first century, the FBI is asking its agents and support personnel to do their jobs without the tools other companies use or that you may use at home on your system."

Email was the FBI's other Achilles' heel. While the world transitioned from paid AOL accounts to free Hotmail accounts, making email ubiquitous, the FBI continued to print memos and route them in interoffice envelopes. For this, at least, there were good reasons. The transition from paper to digital introduced new vulnerabilities that, frankly, terrified the FBI. Before email replaced conference calls and in-person meets—before instant messaging, texting, and tweeting—the FBI had locked information in guarded vaults and gave only a few people the keys. Internet connectivity changed the way we conduct business, how we communicate, and how we gather information. It shrank the earth to the size of a data point and created shared communities between people who previously could never know each other's stories. But it also became the spy's closest companion—and the security expert's nightmare. The FBI and the majority of the intelligence community implemented extraordinary controls that mitigated the dangers posed by an open and accessible Internet. The most classified information remained behind servers that didn't touch the anarchy that we call the World Wide Web.

In the year 2000, though, email had revolutionized world communication, and the FBI had caught the buzz. It was either jump on board or become obsolete. But we still hadn't figured out how email could be integrated into a secure system without compromising that security. The FBI's initial solution was to continue to keep the two separate. Each squad had a single team computer that was exclusively used for the purposes of email. Which meant that everyone used two computers: one internally connected computer to deal with sensitive government work, and a separate, external computer to access the Internet.

Email gained traction as the preferred method of communication, and employees cried for change. The single squad Internet computer created the same problems that any big family living in a smallish house manages every morning: everyone wants to use the bathroom at the same time.

We were all behind the curve, which is why Room 9930 had two computers, both of which had clearly been recycled several times over. I knew that the covert purpose of IA/ST was to catch a spy, but the FBI could have at least given better tech to the team ostensibly tasked with securing the FBI's data.

My chair squeaked beneath my weight. The FBI could have also given us better furniture. I leaned back and forth, making noise the way one might worry a painful tooth. While the dinosaur on my desk booted to an already-outdated version of Windows, I picked up my executive office phone and called Kate.

"I'm here."

"Good. How's it going?"

I shouldered the phone and typed my username and password into the FBI NET prompt. "Fine. I'm just not sure what I'm supposed to be doing here."

A low voice, almost a whisper, made me lose my grip on the phone. "Who are you talking to?" I looked up to see Hanssen looming over me. In the first ten minutes he had already thrown me off my game.

"Sorry, honey, I have to go," I told Kate. "My, ah, new boss just walked into the room." I hung up before she could answer.

"That was my wife, Juliana," I said. Hanssen could dissect a frog without a scalpel. His eyes cut right through me. "First day on the new job, you know."

"It's good that you're married," Hanssen said, and walked out of the office. His feet barely made a whisper of noise on the blue industrial carpet. I couldn't remember the last time someone had snuck up on me.

Hanssen's only other words that day were to tell me he was going out around lunchtime. I dutifully called Kate to let her know the boss had left the SCIF and then counted to ten before leaving myself to shadow him. Within two turns I knew I'd never try to follow him inside FBI HQ again. He knew his way around the building like a man who walks a church labyrinth for an hour's meditation every morning. Numerous employees, mostly on the older side, welcomed Hanssen with friendly waves and the sort of greetings that hid an undertone of *How did you get promoted before me?* If they saw me next and disclosed that fact to anyone, I could compromise the investigation. Not to mention the risk of getting lost again each time he took a blind turn I couldn't follow.

My first day as a crack spy hunter fizzled and died without anything of note to write in my surveillance log. After Hanssen left for the evening with a goodbye dripping with manufactured politeness, I locked up and met Kate a few blocks away.

Our first debrief had a single positive note. I hadn't screwed up. Hanssen had come to the office, met his new staff member, and hadn't yet detected that we'd built an extraordinary mousetrap. Mission accomplished, but I'd have to do better.

Kate drove me to law school, listening silently as I detailed each of my few interactions with Hanssen. As I grabbed my books and stepped out of the car, she said, "Great job, kiddo. Put it all in your log."

Kate wanted written surveillance every day. That meant memorizing everything Hanssen said and did so I could type it out later. As soon as I settled into the last row of my Corporations class, I turned to the back of my notebook and scribbled down everything I could remember. What Hanssen said, whom he met with, what he ate, how he dressed, where we went, and what meetings we set up. Anything he mentioned about computers, or old cases. All his hopes and dreams and past indiscretions. At least the ones I could pry out of him—which, at the moment, numbered zero.

If Professor Wilmarth happened to glance toward the back of his lecture hall, he might have thought I was riveted by his lecture on corporate transactions. I wrote furiously in a black-

and-white composition notebook, but not one word was about piercing the corporate shield or forming subsidiaries. I lost myself in the minutiae of my day, dumping my carefully hoarded memories onto the college-ruled pages before time could steal them. I prayed that Wilmarth didn't call on me.

Turley's Criminal Law class followed a short break spent exchanging a few pleasantries with fellow students at an enterprising coffee shop that stayed open late for the future lawyers. When finally the clock stuck nine and Turley rested his case for the evening, I trudged to the Metro to catch Juliana before she turned in for the night.

I would sometimes find Juliana studying at my desk. She would spread out her books in a small clearing of computer parts and floppy disks. As an evening student, I had time for two classes a semester. Juliana was taking six classes across town at American University with an eye on a business degree. She had rounded out courses in reading and writing with Macroeconomics, Psychology 101, and Russian Studies. Knowing law classes would keep me out late, she also continued her lifetime study of the piano with a private instructor.

"Russian?" I leaned over her shoulder and glanced at the textbook cracked open in a pool of lamplight.

"*Da*," she said.

"Almost done?"

"Maybe enough for tonight." She craned her neck for a kiss. "I'd love a bath."

"I'll heat up some water."

"*Spasibo balshoye.*"

Juliana yawned and left for the tiny bathroom. I filled our biggest pot with water and put it on our two-burner stove. By the time I changed out of my suit into comfortable clothes, the water had boiled.

"Scootch back."

Juliana moved to the back of the tub and shivered in the lukewarm water. The building's pathetic boiler never had enough hot water. Showers required speed and dexterity before the water turned to ice, and warm baths demanded multiple trips to the stove.

Juliana sighed as I poured boiling water at her feet. She stretched into the now-steaming bath and purred her thanks. "How was work?"

I set the heavy pot out in the hall and peeled oven mitts from my hands. "Okay. I met my new boss."

She turned to look at me. "Was he nice?"

"Not exactly."

"How do you mean?"

"We barely spoke two words. I'm not even sure what I'm expected to do."

"Ask him about the Redskins." She laughed. "All you American men love talking football."

"Maybe I will." I picked up the pot.

"Honey," Juliana said, stopping me. "You'll be fine. You always are."

"Thanks," I said.

She pretended to shiver and made big eyes at me. "Maybe another?"

I laughed. "Anything for you."

"Good boy," she said.

I closed the door behind me and quickly set another pot of water to boil. While I waited, I unlocked a drawer in my work desk and removed a laptop the FBI had issued me. I set the blocky netbook on Juliana's Russian textbook and fired up the boot sequence. Before the ancient machine could finish booting, the water boiled.

I donned oven mitts, made another trip to rescue Juliana from hypothermia, and promised her another pot. While the third pot heated up, I snatched my composition notebook out of my shoulder bag and turned to my work. The following evening, I would need to provide a surveillance log to Kate, and I couldn't very well write it and print it out with Hanssen looking over my shoulder.

I slotted a 3.5-inch floppy disk labeled LAW SCHOOL NOTES into the laptop, opened up a Word document, and started writing.

"Eric!"

Juliana's shout nearly made me fall out of my chair. I slammed the laptop shut and spun around in time to catch her dash past me in a dripping bathrobe toward the kitchen. The forgotten pot bubbled scalding water over the stove and onto the floor.

Juliana reached for the pot and then cursed. She glared at me and then at the oven mitts in my hand before thrusting her hand into a stream of cold water from the kitchen sink.

I spared a moment to slip my composition book back into my shoulder bag before rushing the three steps it took to reach the kitchen. The oven mitts hung useless from one hand. As little and late as my apology.

"I'll be fine," Juliana said. "What were you doing over there? Playing video games?"

"I wish," I said honestly. "I wanted to type up some law school notes."

She pushed past me to the freezer and cracked an ice cube from its tray. "On that laptop? When did you get that? We can't afford . . ."

I took the ice cube from her and wrapped it in a paper towel, then took her hand gently and examined the red burn across her palm. "The FBI issued it to me. I'm only supposed to use it for FBI memos, but didn't think anyone would care if I wrote a law school paper on it."

I held the ice against her hand as I told my lie. She leaned her head against my chest. Her wet hair chilled my skin where it soaked through my hoodie.

"I'm going to go get my pajamas on," she said. "Tuck me in."

She left wet footprints in her wake as she retreated to the bedroom. I hid the laptop under the couch and followed more slowly. When I got into the room, Juliana had curled up into a ball under the comforter. I quietly slid in beside her and lent my warmth to hers.

When she relaxed into the measured breathing and tiny movements that told me honest sleep had come, I slipped out of bed and took all four steps to the living room and the laptop under the couch. I typed up my notes, encrypted them, and saved them to the small floppy disk. The following night, I would hand the disk to Kate on the way to law school and she would give me back another one, blank. Each night this would become my routine.

My father used to say that sleep was a weapon. For me, sleep was an adversary.

CHAPTER 6

THE WORST POSSIBLE PLACE

January 17, 2001—Wednesday

Wake up. It's a new day."

Thoughts of murder fled before the smell of freshly brewed coffee. I cracked my eyes to find Juliana smiling at me over my favorite mug. Tendrils of steam curled lazily above a golden FBI seal. I'd bought the mug for myself from the FBI gift shop after receiving my badge and credentials. The fact that a highly classified undercover operative sipped his morning coffee from an official FBI mug was a joke I shared with myself.

Juliana was already dressed in jeans and a startling red blouse. She woke with the sun. I preferred that the sun be in its proper place in the sky before I fell out of bed.

"How is your hand?"

She wiggled her fingers. "Better this morning. Nothing serious."

"I'm sorry."

She smiled. "Get dressed. Breakfast is ready."

We didn't have a table, so we ate on our couch with plates perched on laps. Juliana had woken me up an hour early so that we'd have time together. I couldn't tell her that I'd slept less than four hours. By the time I got my surveillance log finished and skimmed the cases I'd need to know for class, midnight had come and gone.

"The Hello Lady was at it again last night," Juliana said.

I took a bite of my scrambled egg on toast. "She's completely crazy."

"It's a bird. I'm sure of it." Juliana's smug grin made me laugh. "Wanna bet?"

"How can we ever know?"

"Aren't you some sort of FBI investigator?"

I set my empty plate on our tiny coffee table. "The FBI didn't train me to spy on our neighbor!"

"But aren't you curious? You got onto the roof."

I shushed her. I'd picked the lock on the padlock leading up to the roof so we could install a satellite dish and watch more than five TV channels. As far as we knew, no one in the complex knew that I'd dropped a cable over the side of the building and in through one of our windows.

"I only use my powers for good."

She snorted. "Good like fifty-five TV channels we never have time to watch."

"I won't be in law school forever."

She glanced at our clock. "You'll be late for your second day at work. I'll drop you off at the Metro."

A beautiful blonde had woken me up with a cup of coffee, I didn't get lost on the way to 9930, and I'd beat my boss to the office. Not a bad start to the morning. It could only go downhill from here.

The combination lock confounded my first few tries. I hated those locks. So did most FBI personnel. It wasn't uncommon to see a whole squad standing out in the hallway in the morning, waiting for the one guy who knew how to open the thing to arrive. I was not that guy.

"Need help?" Garcia grinned under his thick mustache. As he reached for the combination dial, his blazer gaped, and I saw a holstered gun at his hip. Most veteran agents locked their guns in desks when they arrived at HQ. You could always spot the newbies because they walked around heeled. Garcia was anything but a newbie. It was clear the investigation had us all on edge.

"Open Sesame," he said. The lock clicked and I heard the deadbolts slide home. "You can do the rest. The last number is sticky."

I thanked him and completed the security sequence to enter the SCIF. I felt like the dumb teenager who returns to the haunted house while the audience is screaming for him to run.

"I'm right down the hall," Garcia said, and walked away.

I left everything unlocked and paced the Spartan room. Blank walls and boring furniture. Thin carpet that would set your hair on end if you walked around in socks. Zero windows, one door, baffles on the vents to prevent noise from escaping. Harsh overhead lights beat down relentlessly. A massive whiteboard dominated the wall that Hanssen's office door shared. On a whim, I picked up a black marker and wrote "Information Assurance Security Team" in big letters at the top. Then I underlined it.

The door beeped. *Here we go.*

Hanssen plowed into the room clutching a small cardboard box with one arm and dragging an exercise contraption behind him with the other. He paused and peered past me at the whiteboard.

"Do you want help with the, um, exercise machine, boss?"

"It's a rowing machine," Hanssen said. "I row."

I didn't know what to say to that, so I took a page from Hanssen's book and said nothing. Hanssen set the machine down and strode past me to the whiteboard. He thrust the box at my chest, snatched an eraser from the whiteboard tray, and attacked my markings. He then wrote "Section" after the remaining words.

"Information Assurance Section," I read, and immediately regretted opening my mouth. "Boss, aren't we a security team under Garcia's operations section?"

His withering glance nearly made me drop the box. "We are deciding who we are and what this section will accomplish. Not those paper pushers out there."

"Understood."

"We'll see. Your first task is to define 'Information Assurance.' We need to know what we are doing before we start doing it."

"I'll get right on that."

He peered at me just long enough to push me from uncomfortable to concerned, then took the box from me. "My office." He paused. "Bring the rowing machine."

I followed Hanssen from the bright halogen lights of the main pit area of the SCIF into his gloomy cave. He paused before slumping into the executive chair to pull a thick gray device from his back pocket. My eyes tracked his hand.

"It's a Palm Pilot." He froze, watching me watching him.

I stared at the thick digital assistant and caught the label on the back. A Palm IIIx. "I have a pager," I said through a mouth dried out by my pathetic joke.

He slipped the Palm into the blue canvas bag beside his desk. "And that's why you'll always be a worthless clerk."

The desk lamp illuminated half his face and left the rest of the room adrift in shadows. The analytical part of me wondered if the technical team had tested the hidden camera under lowlight conditions. The rest of me stood like a chastised student before a very angry principal.

Two leather seats waited before my new supervisor's desk. Without asking, I sank into one as a long, uncomfortable silence stretched between us, interrupted only by the machinegun click of Hanssen's ballpoint pen.

I could see the suspicion on his face. Go find your nearest friend from the military, police, or rescue squad—or anyone doing intelligence, special ops, or high-stakes investigative work. Any of them will agree that their work requires them to balance on the razor's edge that separates suspicion from paranoia. Suspicion is healthy. It guards your back, keeps your eyes up and open and alert to signs of danger. Paranoia is suspicion's ugly younger brother. Paranoia paralyzes decision-making, invents threats out of thin air, and crushes all confidence beneath a heavy boot. Right now, Hanssen was suspicious. But any mistake I made—an errant word, a stray slip of paper, a phone call, a feather's touch—could push him over the edge. If this guy really was a spy, he would, at best, cut and run. At worst, he might shoot me on his way out the door.

"So what do you think of the Redskins?" I asked.

There are many ways to unnerve someone. Long periods of uncomfortable silence will often prompt random forays into conversation. I didn't want to talk about the weather, so I took Juliana's advice from the night before and chose my favorite football team. In 2000 the Redskins had fired their coach after winning six of their first eight games. Everyone was still talking about it.

Not Hanssen.

"Football is a gladiator sport," he said with a wave of his pen. "Only idiots and brutes play. You'd have to be just as much of an idiot to watch it."

I hunched back in my chair. My first attempt at conversation had flamed out as spectacularly as the Redskins' season. Hanssen clicked his pen and glared at me.

"Tell me about your wife," he said.

Saying something unexpected in a conversation can also unnerve someone. I didn't want to speak about my personal life with someone who'd done something to get on the wrong side of the FBI. But alone in the room with Hanssen, I didn't have a choice.

"She's from Germany," I said. "We were married in August." I forced a smile. "It's all very new."

"Where in Germany?" His voice sounded less robotic, more pleasant.

"The far east. You wouldn't know her hometown. I couldn't even find it on a map."

"You'd be surprised what I know." Hanssen sat back. "Does she speak Russian?"

"Yes." I wanted to lie, but how much did he already know?

"Interesting," Hanssen said, leaning back, his stare unmoving.

Before the fall of the Berlin Wall, the Allied Forces controlled the west side of Germany and built it into a country of peace, democracy, and prosperity; Russia, however, controlled the east. The machine-gun turrets on the east side of the Berlin Wall had faced inward, toward their own population. Russian socialization began as early as possible, and every child learned Russian as a second language. Juliana's English schoolbook was filled with anti-Western propaganda. Although churches speckled the countryside, the Socialist Party frowned upon religion and reached the barest accommodation with the dominant Protestant faith. Each house in Juliana's village was a compound. High walls and wooden shutters blocked neighbors who might report to the local Stasi. The government stole acres of land from Juliana's grandfather, and neighbors hesitated to accept her half-Polish mother.

When the Berlin Wall finally came crashing down in 1989, and David Hasselhoff united the east and west in song, Juliana had just turned twelve. By 1994, under the "Two Plus Four" Treaty signed by East and West Germany and the four Allied Forces, all foreign troops had to depart the now-unified country. Russia shuffled more than 485,000 soldiers and dependents, along with thousands of tanks, armored personnel carriers, artillery pieces, planes, and helicopters, back across the Russian border. Germany's two halves might have reunited, but the east suffered a recession that sparked a migration of young professionals to the west. Juliana left her small village the moment she could. Her first job was in Aachen, Germany—over 800 kilometers directly west from the town of her birth. A year later, she found a program that would take her to the United States, farther west than anyone in her village had ever traveled.

Hanssen clicked his pen, his pupils as round as bullet heads in the dim light. "Do you know what we are doing here?"

"Protecting information?" I ventured.

Hanssen sighed with disgust. "Where on earth did they find you?"

My mask slipped, and I could feel microexpressions colonize my face. "I'm an investigator," I said, forcing myself back to neutral. "Years on a terrorism squad ghosting targets. Two years ago when I started law school, I transferred to computer analytical work." I thought it best to leave out the years I spent tracking spies.

Hanssen scooped up his pen and wrote a single word on a yellow legal pad: "Investigator."

"We are protecting every data system in the FBI—FBI NET, ACS, Trusted Guard, our data center—all of it." The pen whirled and clicked. "Take the Automated Case System, for example. Complete garbage. All it would take is one bad bureau person to invalidate the security. ACS works as long as someone is not a spy."

As of 2018, the FBI has jurisdiction over violations of more than 200 categories of federal crimes; employs 35,000 people; and staffs 56 field offices throughout the United States, more than 400 resident agencies in smaller cities and towns, and more than 60 international offices called "legal attachés" in US embassies worldwide. In other words, the FBI is massive, and it does a lot of things. The FBI relied on ACS to share immediate information between squads. It sought to solve the problem of FBI SWAT agents kicking in the front door of a drug-cooking operation while, unbeknownst to them, an FBI organized crime task force stormed the back door. Worst-case scenario? Top FBI marksmen fire at each other while the bad guys cower in the middle of the raid site with their hands over their heads.

To add to the complications, the FBI is not the only agency that conducts counterintelligence and counterterrorism operations, or chases spies, or deals with corruption, crime, and kidnapping. Tens of thousands of civilian law-enforcement personnel across the DEA, CIA, NSA, Secret Service, ATF, and others all have a stake in the game of defending the United States from domestic and external threats. For this reason, the FBI shares certain case information with other agencies as well.

Hanssen made a good point. Sharing information works only as long as no one gives access to a spy. He clicked the pen. The noise had grown past a distraction. Each press of his thumb drove a nail into the side of my head.

"I heard you attend George Washington Law School," he said, a switchback turn. "I have a nephew who graduated from there. My son is in law school at Notre Dame."

I grabbed the lifeline and pulled my way back into the normal rhythm of conversation. We learned that our mothers share the same name—Vivian. Both of our fathers served in the Navy when we were born. Hanssen's father had then become a Chicago police officer. My grandfather walked the beat in Queens, New York. Commonality. The more I could find in common with the guy, the better I could do my job and chip away at him. I sat forward and fought against the smile that tickled the edge of my lips. Maybe I could do this. Hanssen was known to be discreet, to keep to himself. He rarely spoke to people, and he made those who spoke to him feel inferior, turning them off from further conversation. If he went to a party, no one remembered him. If he walked up to a craps table, the next throw would seven out. He was the ultimate cooler. He had the perfect demeanor for a spy.

The detail-oriented, analytical FBI had chosen me over countless senior agents with decades of experience in making people talk. I had no idea why, but maybe they'd put me in this chair across from Hanssen's desk because they knew I had something that the undercover superstars didn't. Maybe *I* was the superstar.